W9-CAN-909

REMOVED
from Collection

11/13/14

Louisburg Library District No. 1

206 S. Broadway

Louisburg, KS. 66053

913-837-2217

www.louisburglibrary.org

The UNDERGROUND RAILROAD

By Michael Rajczak

Gareth Stevens
Publishing

Louisburg Library
Bringing People and Information Together

Please visit our website, www.garethstevens.com. For a free color catalog of all our high-quality books, call toll free 1-800-542-2595 or fax 1-877-542-2596.

Library of Congress Cataloging-in-Publication Data

Rajczak, Michael.
The Underground Railroad / by Michael Rajczak.
 p. cm. — (What you didn't know about history)
Includes index.
ISBN 978-1-4824-0603-0 (pbk.)
ISBN 978-1-4824-0604-7 (6-pack)
ISBN 978-1-4824-0601-6 (library binding)
1. Underground Railroad — Juvenile literature. 2. Fugitive slaves — United States — History — 19th century — Juvenile literature. I. Rajczak, Michael. II. Title.
E450.R35 2014
973.7115—dc23

First Edition

Published in 2014 by
Gareth Stevens Publishing
111 East 14th Street, Suite 349
New York, NY 10003

Copyright © 2014 Gareth Stevens Publishing

Designer: Andrea Davison-Bartolotta
Editor: Kristen Rajczak

Photo credits: Cover, p. 1 Charles T. Webber/Wikimedia Commons; pp. 5 (inset), 17 Stock Montage/Getty Images; p. 5 (main) Universal History Archive/Getty Images; p. 6 Chicago History Museum/UIG/Getty Images; p. 7 (main) Hulton Archive/Getty Images; p. 7 (inset) Oleksii Iezhov/Shutterstock.com; pp. 9, 12 Kean Collection/Getty Images; pp. 11, 19 (both) MPI/Getty Images; pp. 13 (all), 15 Ohio Historical Society/American Memory/Library of Congress; p. 16 courtesy of the Library of Congress; p. 21 Dr_Flash/Shutterstock.com.

All rights reserved. No part of this book may be reproduced in any form without permission in writing from the publisher, except by a reviewer.

Printed in the United States of America

CPSIA compliance information: Batch #CW14GS: For further information contact Gareth Stevens, New York, New York at 1-800-542-2595.

CONTENTS

Library District No. 1
Louisburg Library
206 S. Broadway
Louisburg, KS 66053

Words in the glossary appear in **bold** type the first time they are used in the text.

WHAT WAS THE UNDERGROUND RAILROAD?

Most people know of the former slave Harriet Tubman. Before the **American Civil War**, she helped others escape slavery as part of the Underground Railroad.

"Underground Railroad" is a term for all the **routes** slaves took to reach freedom in the North. It was a huge network of people and places. But in order for slaves to use this network, they often had to travel hundreds of miles. Slaves from border states were much more likely to make the journey successfully than those from farther south.

Did You Know?

One story says a slave catcher was the first to use the term "Underground Railroad" when a slave he was chasing seemed to disappear. He said it was as though the slave disappeared on an underground railroad!

The name "Underground Railroad" stuck, perhaps because of the railroad **vocabulary** used to talk about the big network. Conductors were those who helped guide the slaves, while the safe places they hid were called stations.

The United States in 1857

Free States
Slave States
Not decided

5

THE CRUEL LIFE OF A SLAVE

It's no wonder slaves wanted to escape. They had to do whatever they were told. Most slaves worked planting and harvesting crops. They were given little food and cheap clothing, and lived in shabby shacks. Slaves were treated as property, not people.

If slaves disobeyed or tried to run away, they were beaten and whipped. Some were **branded** with a hot iron. Fingers or toes would be cut off. Even worse for some slaves, owners could sell family members, often separating parents and children.

slave tag

Did You Know?

Seventy-five percent of the people in the South didn't own slaves. Most people who did own slaves owned 20 or fewer.

Slaves who tried to run away or argued with their master were forced to wear iron **shackles** like these. Other slaves were warned against acting out by being forced to watch whippings.

7

How it Began

Historians believe Isaac T. Hopper, a Quaker, began establishing safe places for slaves to hide around 1787. Some who joined this network were white **abolitionists**, but over time, most of the conductors of the Underground Railroad were escaped slaves themselves!

Abolitionists weren't all supportive of the Underground Railroad. Many didn't want to break the law, even though it meant fighting against slavery. The Quakers were commonly against slavery, too, but they also wanted to find legal ways to fight and end slavery.

Did You Know?

Many slaves escaped alone. Reaching the border between the free states and the slave states was hard because they often didn't know the land they had to travel.

Most slaves wouldn't have known the Underground Railroad by name. It was a term mostly used in the North.

FINDING THE ROUTES

Over time, enough safe places were known so that there were many different ways to get to Ohio and Pennsylvania, where slavery was outlawed. There weren't permanent, established routes, however. People hunting for escaped slaves would have caught on too easily!

Once a slave reached the North, the Underground Railroad could help them hide. At first, **penalties** for helping runaway slaves were lightly enforced, especially in northern states. But in 1850, a new **fugitive** slave law increased fines and jail time for those helping escaped slaves.

Did You Know?

The Fugitive Slave Act of 1850 made it legal for southern slave hunters to search for and bring back runaway slaves from free northern states. They could claim any black person they saw was an escaped slave!

Up to 100,000 people may have escaped slavery in the South before the Civil War. That might seem like a lot, but in 1860, there were as many as 4 million slaves in the United States!

PLACES TO HIDE

What was it like hiding along the Underground Railroad? Uncomfortable!

"Station masters" built hidden places in their homes and barns to hide runaways. Cupboards with hinges revealed small spaces that could hide a few people. Rugs on the floor carefully disguised trapdoors to secret cellars. After the Fugitive Slave Act of 1850 passed, these hiding places had to be even better. If a slave hunter tried to search a place, hidden runaways had to be absolutely silent. Hiding places were dark and very stuffy.

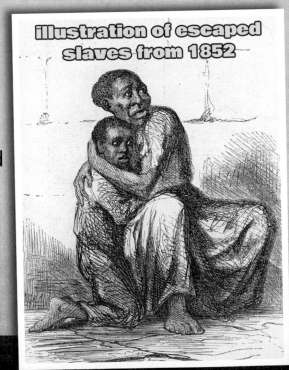

illustration of escaped slaves from 1852

This set of stairs reaches from the Ohio River to a well-known stop along the Underground Railroad. The steps may not have been built until the 1900s, but the house at the top was known as a safe place many years before.

$150 REWARD.

RANAWAY from the subscriber, on the night of Monday the 11th July, a negro man named

TOM,

about 30 years of age, 5 feet 6 or 7 inches high; of dark color; heavy in the chest; several of his jaw teeth out; and upon his body are several old marks of the whip, one of them straight down the back. He took with him a quantity of clothing, and several hats.

A reward of $150 will be paid for his apprehension and security, if taken out of the State of Kentucky; $100 if taken in any county bordering on the Ohio river; $50 if taken in any of the interior counties except Fayette; or $20 if taken in the latter county.

july 12-84-tf   B. L. BOSTON.

100 DOLLARS
REWARD!

Ranaway from the subscriber on the 27th of July, my Black Woman, named

EMILY,

Seventeen years of age, well grown, black color, has a whining voice. She took with her one dark calico and one blue and white dress, a red corded gingham bonnet; a white striped shawl and slippers. I will pay the above reward if taken near the Ohio river on the Kentucky side, or THREE HUNDRED DOLLARS, if taken in the State of Ohio, and delivered to me near Lewisburg, Mason County, Ky.   THO'S. H. WILLIAMS.

August 4, 1853.

reward notices for runaway slaves

DESTINATION CANADA

Once runaway slaves reached Lake Erie, Lake Ontario, or the Niagara River, they needed a way to cross into Canada, where slavery was illegal. A man named Josiah Tryon used his family's home on the Niagara River as one such place. It had several basements for slaves to hide in!

In Ohio, Robbins Burrell would cover runaways with vegetables or hay and drive them in a wagon to Lorain, Ohio. There they would be smuggled aboard boats for the trip across Lake Erie.

Did You Know?

During the winter, the Ohio River would freeze over in spots, allowing runaways to cross over to Ohio from present-day West Virginia and Kentucky.

Smuggling slaves across Lake Erie was often dangerous.

OTHER ROUTES

The Underground Railroad wasn't only made up of escape routes north. During the 1700s, several runaways hid with the Seminole tribe in Florida. One group of runaways made their way to Andros Island in the Bahamas. Once Mexico abolished slavery, slaves—especially those from Texas—headed there.

Between Virginia and North Carolina is a big swamp where some escaped slaves hid. Even the boldest slave hunters often turned back, unable to cross the rough conditions of the swamp.

IN THE SWAMP.

Slaves found many ways to escape slavery, and all were risky. A slave named Henry Brown hid in a wooden box and had himself shipped from Virginia to Philadelphia, Pennsylvania.

Did You Know?

Ellen Craft wrapped herself in bandages and disguised herself as an injured white man and said her husband, William, was "his" slave. They were able to travel openly on a train from Georgia to Philadelphia!

CONDUCTORS

Underground Railroad conductors had to have good knowledge of the land and the location of safe houses. Some became famous for their efforts. History has forgotten the names of thousands of others.

Former slave John Parker, along with his white neighbor John Rankin, transported runaways across the Ohio River. Both of their homes were Underground Railroad stations. A free black man named William Still who lived in Philadelphia, Pennsylvania, helped many escaped slaves get to Canada. For others, he found jobs and homes in the city.

Did-You-Know?

Runaways ate whatever was offered and whatever they could find or steal along the way. Often they went hungry.

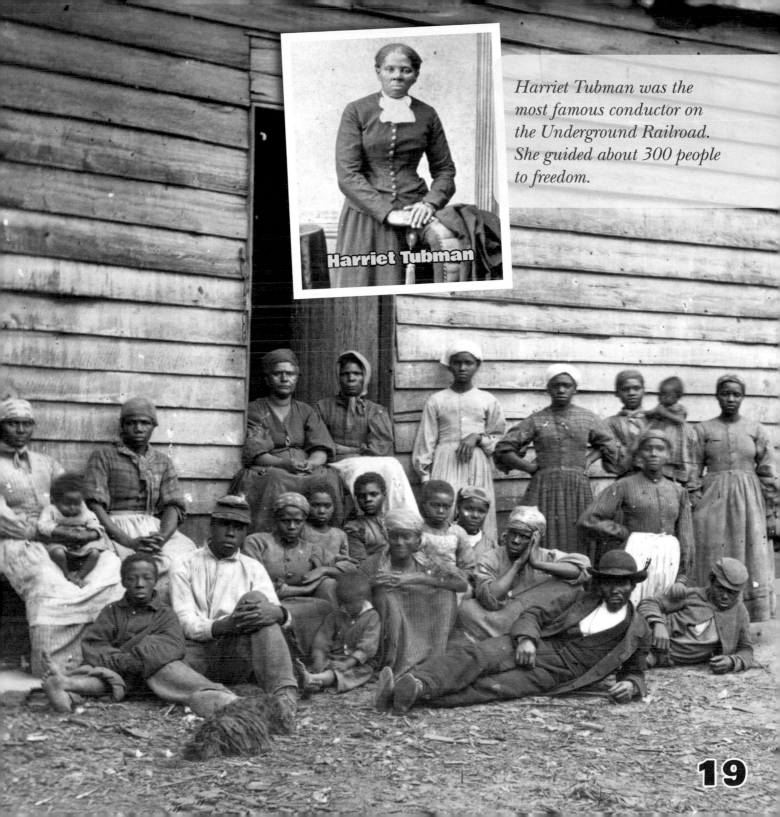

Harriet Tubman was the most famous conductor on the Underground Railroad. She guided about 300 people to freedom.

Harriet Tubman

NEW LIVES

At the end of their journeys, escaped slaves tried to start new lives. The Quakers in Canada bought 800 acres (324 ha) of land to establish a community for former slaves.

Unfortunately, newly freed slaves weren't very welcome in northern US states. The Underground Railroad could help them leave slavery behind, but not **prejudice**. They had a hard time getting jobs and weren't paid well when they did. Most were forced to live separately from whites. Some communities placed limits on the freedoms and rights of former slaves.

Did You Know?

There were **riots** in some northern cities over allowing black children into public schools.

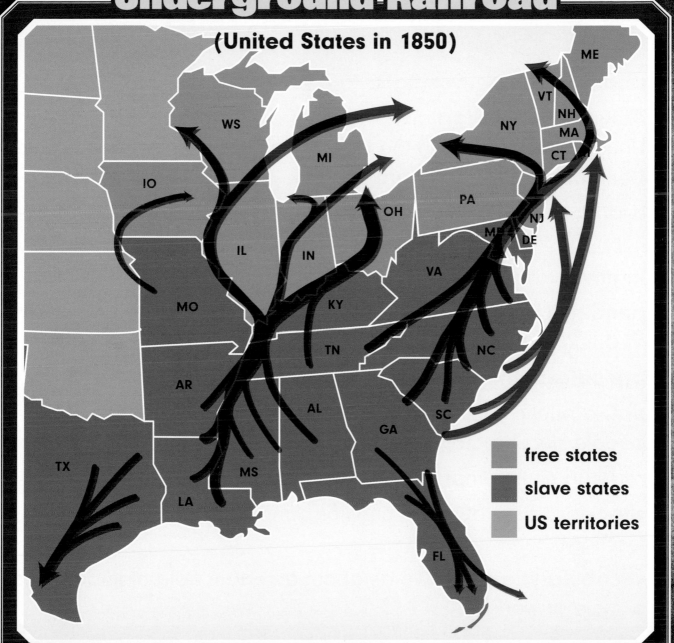

Routes of the Underground Railroad

(United States in 1850)

free states
slave states
US territories

21

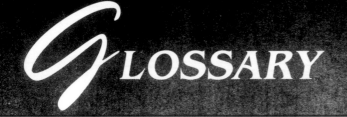

GLOSSARY

abolitionist: one who fights to end slavery

American Civil War: a war fought from 1861 to 1865 in the United States between the Union (the Northern states) and the Confederacy (the Southern states)

brand: to burn a letter or shape into a person's skin using a hot iron

fugitive: running away

penalty: the pain or loss someone must go through as a result of doing something wrong

prejudice: a negative attitude directed toward a group

riot: a public disturbance during which a group of angry people become noisy and out of control

route: a course that people travel

shackles: a set of metal rings or bands that holds hands or feet together

vocabulary: a set of words about a certain field of knowledge or type of work

FOR MORE INFORMATION

Books

Ford, Carin T. *The Underground Railroad and Slavery Through Primary Sources.* Berkeley Heights, NJ: Enslow, 2013.

McConaghy, Lorraine, and Judy Bentley. *Free Boy: A True Story of Slave and Master.* Seattle, WA: University of Washington Press, 2013.

Senker, Cath. *Who Traveled the Underground Railroad?* Chicago, IL: Capstone Heinemann Library, 2014.

Websites

Interactive Map: The Underground Railroad
eduplace.com/kids/socsci/books/applications/imaps/maps/g5s_u6/
Use this map to answer questions about the routes of the Underground Railroad.

The Underground Railroad: Escape from Slavery
teacher.scholastic.com/activities/bhistory/underground_railroad/
Learn even more about the Underground Railroad on Scholastic's interactive website.

Publisher's note to educators and parents: Our editors have carefully reviewed these websites to ensure that they are suitable for students. Many websites change frequently, however, and we cannot guarantee that a site's future contents will continue to meet our high standards of quality and educational value. Be advised that students should be closely supervised whenever they access the Internet.